Table of Contents

Introduction

A billionaire, a super-genius investor, a philanthropist, and an entrepreneur, Warren Buffett, is the second richest person, after Bill Gates, in the United States; and the fourth richest globally. Behind his demeanor, he is one of America's toughest businessmen. With his excellent time management skills, Warren Buffet has succeeded to come by his money in a truthful way, leaving an evident impact in peoples' lives and his life as a whole. If Warren Buffet is a big enchilada, then a lot more little enchiladas under him have and are becoming rich too! He is known for his philanthropic moves, where he is linked up to quite a number of charity donations, giving a handsome portion of his fortune to people and even organizations. Nevertheless, besides his philanthropic nature, he opts for the value for his dollars in his expenditure.

Apparently, Warren Buffett began investing at a tender age when he was just 11 years, when he bought share in the Apple Company. It was clear to him that in years to come, he would be very rich. At the age of 13 years, Buffett had started his own business as a paperboy. In this business, as a paperboy, he used to sell his horse racing tip sheets.

Presently, Buffett is the CEO and Chairman of Berkshire Hathaway, which is a Multinational Corporation that has a net worth of $162 billion in revenues as of the year 2015. He is arguably one of the most famous and successful businessman in history. If you had invested ten thousand dollars in the early 1966, today you would be three hundred million dollars rich. He has become famous in life because of:

- His businesses;
- Investments in stocks;
- Money (currently worth over $60 billion);
- His moral and ethical values;
- His philanthropic nature.

Buffett is a real philanthropist that has pledged to give away to charity, nearly all his wealth. He has pledged to give 99% of his wealth to charity, having pledged to give the most charitable gift in human history, to the Bill and Melinda Gates foundation, that totaled to approximately 83% of his wealth. Throughout his business and entrepreneurial life, Buffett has generously shared valuable thoughts on business and life. We can also learn a lot of lessons from how he handles his charitable ventures and essentially his investments, money and life. The following are the top 20 lessons for business and life success instances that we can grasp from Warren Buffett's shared experiences.

Life Lessons:

Lesson # 1: Have a Margin of Safety in Life

Life has to be polished by hardships here and there. Life is a journey and you can neither live it without ups nor downs. In your day-to-day endeavors, a lot of changes in terms of growth take place, as everybody definitely has to grow in various dimensions. Basically, people evolve and these implies to their support systems, which are full of constant changes. These changes apply to all kinds of races, from rich to poor, young to old, weak to tough no matter what kind of life style a person lives. Interestingly, they are absolutely unavoidable to all! Nobody is exceptional in the hustle and tussles of life.

Over your business and employment life, you will encounter various misfortunes and stumbling blocks. Some of them can be avoided, while others cannot be avoided in any way. It is an experience that majority of investors, including Warren Buffett, have encountered once in a while in their career. It really frightens when you become suspicious of a difficult or depressing situation, that you have seen coming your direction. However, a depressing state is neither a sickness nor accident, it is a human passage that almost every being is at an equal position to undergo ones in a while. Some people are concerned trying to understand depression in details, but quite a number are working out their best way to leverage the situation such as having a margin of safety in life as a backup.

When the goings get tough for instance that time you have been impeached from your position in a company, similarly when your business is recording losses, and again when your company is downsizing, you will need a substantial amount of capital to cater for your expenditures at home and while getting yourself another deal or employment position.

Key Takeaway:

Warren Buffett is used to securing himself with a substantial amount of money that could adequately cover his expenditures when his businesses are not recording profits. This "margin of safety" provides him with some protection when the going is getting tough. It also acts as a preservation of capital. In his life, Warren, kept distance from war street speculations. As a matter of fact he avoided the war street itself.

Next Action Plan:

Whether you are just a student who is about to hit the job or business market after school, or you are a starter entrepreneur, it is always advisable to secure yourself with a substantial amount of money for an emergency. If you are currently employed, take a small percentage of your salary, it can be even 7%, and secure it in a savings account. Nevertheless, ensure that you can access the account anytime you need this money. It is not advisable to cash it into your lock saving account. Warren Buffet had saved at least $10000 when he was done with school. The value for your own financial power should focus on you. You might be in a business platform or even employed, but the most important is depended on what you do in future. Securing your future financial power, gives you an assurance to be able to support yourself independently in case of hardships in your future life. Everybody has energy to do great things. If you cannot do great things, you have a chance to do small things in a great way.

Some of the holdbacks that prevent you from utilizing your potential are lack of education, which is quite rare in this century. You need to have considerable knowledge pertaining the kind of investment you indulge in or a good understanding of your financial power. Secondly, and most essentially, the kind of habits you develop. Intelligence, integrity and energy are three must have factors that will ensure you have extraordinary results. The three factors are mutually dependent of each other. If you omit intelligence for example, integrity and energy would not apply and would leave you operating below your full potential. To add on top, work out things when you are young, with full energy and commitment.

To sum up, avoid unnecessary debts, which you cannot pay, as this would ensure no progress in your daily endeavors. An example is credit card spending. With credit card expenditure, you are sure of paying back 20%

extra, thereby preventing progress and increasing your general expenditure preventing you from having a margin of safety in the end.

Lesson # 2: Your Past Is Your Best Competitor

Natasha Lyonne says, if you compare yourself to somebody you think is a peer, you can totally loose the plot, and not understand that you are nothing like them in the first place, and that it was never you versus anybody. Many people get it wrong in life when it comes to competition. In most cases, they tend to compete much with their fellow employees, business ventures, and friends, thus, ending up forgetting that their primary goal should have been making their future better than their past, with the help of the present time. Commonly, we tend to look at the people we admire or want to be like, in order to get their secrets that we probably perceive they have, and we lack. On the contrary, you are your own competitor. Eminently, your best competitor is you in your past, and today you ought to outdo your past a great deal. We can spend a lot of our precious time concerned with what people surrounding us do. Besides, we can be pushed to even rate ourselves against them in many things for example in wealth, business, social lives and generally the kind of life styles we should be living. It all lies within us. A procedural change in your past works best; since you are competing with one person and that is you. Most importantly, your biggest rival is who you were in your past.

Warren Buffett understands that it is vital to have a competitive advantage over other businesses. A competitive advantage is a kind of advantage over your competitors that you gain by offering the consumer a greater value. Competitive advantage can be obtained by providing greater service and benefits that will justify the higher prices. The improvement of your service procedurally, is a bold step in ensuring evident improvements in your sales rather than focusing on your competitor's level at a given time. A new day requires a newer version of your ideas yesterday. The ideas applied yesterday were well applicable for that day, but today demands for fresher versions of the ideas. Comparing yourself to your peers would barely give you efficient answers, and neither a keen watch on your competitor would even provide a clear thinking space to get solutions.

"Capitalism is all about somebody coming in and trying to take the castle. Now what you need is a castle that has durable competitive advantage" – *Warren Buffett.*

Key Takeaway:

We can learn from Buffett that knowing your competition is far much better than knowing yourself. Although, you will also learn that Buffett tries to make the present product and services better than the past. In this way, he is pretty sure of an upward variance, compared to the previous attempt. Buffet always had a clear history of where he has come from and where he is headed to. He competes with his past and as a result, he always had a way of convincing himself that he was making forward steps, rather than gathering plentiful of information on competitors, which would arguably slug or confuse his growth and development plan.

Interestingly, Buffett still lives in the house that he lived 41 years ago. In his life, he rarely focused on what his competitors were doing. Many billionaires are living in million dollar houses out there. Buffett's decision to stay in the same house is not driven or determined by his competition toward competitors, but rather, his self being.

Next Action Plan:

Do you have a ridged checklist of the procedures to succeed in your endeavors? Well the brilliantly composed ideas that made you succeed yesterday, will not take you to the next level. For a new day, you surely need fresh ideas relative to your position yesterday. Today is a new day and does not require the ideas that messed you up yesterday. Undertake new ideas rather than becoming ridged on your old perceptions. Simply grasp the inspirations of the people you admire, and use them to create your personal terms, but it is not advisable to literally follow their actions. You will get misled!

You should understand that you work, do business, get an education, and have dreams for the sole purpose of making your life and lives of those who depend on you better. Hence, to succeed in life, you should always strive to better your present and future by benchmarking yourself with your past.

Today you sell $100,000 in revenue and thus you can afford a middle-class restaurant; focus on how to sell $1 million in revenue so as to afford a high-end restaurant.

Lesson # 3: Give Unconditional Love

Mr. Buffett revealed, in his profile for "The Great Minds of Investing," that his father gave him useful lessons when he was young. He states that one of the most important lesson gotten in his life is the lesson about unconditional love. He further goes ahead to say that the unconditional love that he got from his father is the bedrock of his current success in business, entrepreneurship, and life. His father was actually giving the love lessons by example. As much as one makes mistakes, does not imply that it is over and that they should be bonded with their mistakes. Giving unconditional love basically requires that, even after a terrible mistake has occurred, you can still allow the victim back with no strings attached or looking back at their mistakes.

Buffett has outspokenly stated, severally, that his father believed in him. He got support and love from him, Howard Buffett, who was a United States Congressman.

"My dad believed in me, whatever I did, he was all for it. It didn't matter how much money I made or anything like that. It was just, 'Do your best in whatever you take on." Mr. Buffett explained in one of his speeches.

Key Takeaway:

We can learn from Mr. Buffett that loving unconditionally is one of the greatest virtues, which you ought to possess. When you give unconditional love to friends, colleagues and family members, most likely you will also receive unconditional love in return. That is why Buffett remembers, honors and quotes his father until today – because of the unconditional love that he got from him. It was adorable and impacting. And he adds that it is the best thing that a father or mother would give to his or her child.

Next Action Plan:

You should learn the art of loving unconditionally. Love your friends, colleagues, kids and parents without limits. As such, your life becomes better. You get support and love from them. This act instills a spirit of success in you. Similarly, back at home in your family, if you wake up one morning and show love to your wife by wishing her a good morning, just before you both get to your daily duties, the created impact is so much effective to both of you. You will tend to feel the magical feeling of love increasing more than before. This is basically the power of unconditional love.

Showing love to your team and staffs even after they have made mistakes here and there, gives them a sense of confidence to work comfortably and perfectly. A tensed employee would easily make silly mistakes, not because he or she is incompetent, but due to the kind of atmosphere you instill in them when you do not show unconditional love. Buffett has always valued the power created by the virtue of unconditional love, "I mean, there is no power on earth like unconditional love. And I think that if you offered that to your child, I mean, you're 90 percent of the way home. There may be days when you don't feel like it—it's not uncritical love; that's a different animal— but to know you can always come back, that is huge in life. That takes you a long, long way. And I would say that every parent out there that can extend that to their child at an early age, it's going to make for a better human being," were his actual words in an interview by Yahoo news and Huffington Post when he was asked the best advice that he had ever received. The impact created by giving unconditional love, magically alters a person's perception towards issues. He or she becomes positive and finds him or herself reflecting the love back to you.

Lesson # 4: Find Your Personality

Personality can be explained as similar but differing characteristics of a person or people at larger angle. We are all humans with a uniform nature, but each being varies in his or her own way depending on various determining factors. Experience differentiates us altogether. Styles of thought, feelings, and behavior clearly distinguishes one personality to another.

One unique thing with Warren Buffett, is the fact that he doesn't like meetings. Although, he manages his investments and builds his businesses in line with his personality that makes him unique from many established investors.

Buffett undertakes his activities in life, businesses, and entrepreneurship in the way that he enjoys and prefers. Amongst his renowned personalities, he is humble and reachable. He has a combination of particular personality qualities, which facilitate greatness and success, which ideally tend to be magical. The following are some of the most surprising psychological aspects to Warren Buffet's character, which lead to a combination of creating the perfect mindset for running a successful business **life** smoothly.

1. **Independent Thinking**

While it is extremely important to have connections like family, friends and other significant people in your life, the ability of being self-sufficient and in charge of your own life is good. Warren Buffet remains his own self-unmoved by people. May it be important people, vocal people or great number of people? Just as one person once said that the strongest man is he who stands alone and those who fly solo have the strongest wings, Warren Buffett says that a public opinion poll is no supernumerary for thought. He thinks individualistically and he is one of those rare individuals who will stem the sentiments of others so that theirs can transpire. Struggling for independence is a substantial element of normal life where there is a perpetual pull to acclimate, it entirely results into a different alliance, when applied in business or investing environment. One may feel susceptible in investing environment since it is an orientation towards a visualized future. But, Warren Buffett remains in his stand, unmoved.

2. **Modesty**

Modesty is the quality or state of being unassuming or moderate in the estimation of one's abilities. When it comes to acknowledging the role that Warren Buffett plays in some things, which are significantly big, he is characteristically modest.

3. **Conscience.**

The way we judge ourselves taking in considerations our failures and success is what is referred to as conscience. Just as Winston Churchill said, "success is moving from failure to failure without loss of enthusiasm" Warren Buffett's spirit of conscience is exactly in this way. Which helps him to do by himself the right things and learn from his mistakes. Having such a conscience gives one the motivation of moving forward, while taking seriously the ability to make the right decisions and empowering the ability to convalesce from the mistakes one did.

4. Frugality.

This is the act of self-denial or restraining yourself. It is about restraining your compulsions from things that might appear glamorous before you. In today's day-to-day operations, increased desires and consumptions make the act of restraining or self-denial very rare. This virtue of frugality has helped Warren Buffett to accumulate more and more wealth.

5. Deferring gratification.

This is actually the act of foregoing consumption so as one will have more to consume in future. One is required to have certain strength in his character so as to contain precipitateness and anxiety, which are both ultimate weaknesses in any investor such as Warren Buffett.

6. Greed.

This is the act of getting more and more and more. The desire of getting more and more rich has helped Warren Buffett. Just as Mae West said "too much of a good thing can be wonderful" For you to be a renowned successful investor, you need to have the lust of getting more and more good things. Thus, one should be a cheerful greedy. The danger of greed is that it can rob one the chance of enjoying what he or she has.

<u>Key Takeaway:</u>

Just like Warren Buffett, you should find your productive mode. Find your sweet spot and your pace. Buffett understands that by finding his real personality, he will be productive both in business and life. He, therefore, lives a happy life without 'FAKING' anything so as to please those who are around him.

<u>**Next Action Plan:**</u>

You should learn that you are very productive when you find what works best for you. If you are still schooling while undertaking a part-time side job, find a job that fulfills your desire. A job that will help you in building your vision and mission in life and further explore and recognize your personality.

If you are employed or in business, learn to work in line with your personality. You should not go miles out of your personality just to please other people. By so doing, you are assured of success in life

Lesson #5: Keep a Low Profile

Albert Einstein once said, *"The monotony and solitude of a quiet life stimulates the creative mind."* Keeping low profile means behaving in a way that does not attract attention to yourself. It ensures that you have less to spend. Many people will expect Warren Buffett to travel in fancy cars, fancy private jets, and always enjoy spending most of his time in expensive high-end restaurants. Although, Buffett is different!

He lives an incredibly simple lifestyle, considering his status in the society and world in general. At times, Buffett does his best to circumvent the public eye. He regularly gives opinions on public and economic policies, although he avoids the extreme behavior that indicates he is ultra-successful.

Warren Buffett understands that his prosperity comes from the success and flourishing of his investments and businesses. Hence, he goes miles ahead to keep a low profile when it comes to his personal life. He therefore avoids participation in anything that will draw more attention to him rather than his businesses, like proactive public comments.

<u>**Key Takeaway:**</u>

There are ways that would enable you maintain a low profile in life. Some of these ways to help you keep a low profile like successful people are:

- **Keep a small amount of pious friends.**

It is essential for one to have friends in life. It is equally important for you to keep few friends who will come in your aid while you are in need because; a friend in need is a friend indeed. Rather than when one keeps friend who are unhelpful; they tend to spill his secrets and let him known to the public.

- **Conceal your good deeds.**

It is not heroic for one to go out telling everyone what he or she has achieved. Just as people will tend to conceal their bad deeds, it is good for you to conceal your good deeds. It is not good for you to lift up yourself or to speak of your praise, since the more fame a person gets, the more opposition he or she gets.

- **Make strong intentions**

The stronger your intentions are, the more you will attain your goals. Keep yourself and your life to yourself. Do not let it be known by others.

- **Mind your own business**

Always focus on the things affecting in your life and change them if you cannot accept them or accept them if you cannot change them, instead of being concerned with what other people are doing in their lives. This will give you a chance to concentrate on improving your life and your business, if you are an investor or an entrepreneur. People will precisely be less likely to bring dramas or gossip about you since they will not be having any clue on how your life style looks like.

- **Deal with conflict quietly and gracefully.**

When you are a low-profile maintaining person it is hard for you to find yourself amidst of conflict with others since you don't interfere with their lifestyle. But sometimes, the conflicts are inventible. When such situations arise, it is always advisable for you try and keep calm and maintain kindness. Try to solve the disagreement in an orderly manner, or even try to be open to compromise and appeasing to the other party, so long as you are fine with it and it does not violate your behavior and values. By doing this, you will not attract much attention like the one who solves a problem with a problem.

Hence helping you keep your profile low.

By keeping a low profile, Buffett can focus on his businesses and investments rather than the attention that would have otherwise come with a lavish lifestyle. He will, therefore, spend less time clarifying comments that he made on his opinions since they aren't divisive nor wild. His life is also his personal business.

Next Action Plan:

Whether or not you are into investing, you can learn a lot from Buffett when it comes to keeping a low profile in life. You should steer clear exposing everything that you do in your life on social media. You should avoid unnecessary public attention. By so doing, you will make your life simple and thereby be able to focus on your job or business using the above ways.

Lesson # 6: Simplicity Works Wonders

Simplicity is the quality or condition of being easy to understand. Buffett avoids venturing in exotic investments at all cost. He otherwise prefers keeping his investments simple – which earns him a lot of money in return.

"Derivatives are financial weapons of mass destruction. " – Warren Buffett

He avoids stocks from social media companies because they are not readily measurable as they are new business concepts. He understands basic things like insurance and famous Coca-Cola companies.

Buffett circumvents putting his money into industries and companies that he knows nothing about. His billions and simple yet healthy lifestyle resulted from investing in what he is aware of.

Key Takeaway:

You can learn that Buffett's life becomes dull because he ventures on investments that he understands and know. He can deal with both tough economic times and good economic times when it comes to his businesses and investments.

<u>**Next Action Plan:**</u>

You should invest and work in what you understand and know. Steer clear with business ventures or job opportunities that you don't know, no matter how they are paying. By so doing, you will make your life simpler during tough times. Dealing with what you know is much easier than what you aren't aware of.

In business, simplicity is golden. To embrace simplicity, limit your objectives and strategies. We know very well that without a target, we cannot be able to achieve the desires of life. So for one to be successful, it is Important for him or her to have a target or a strategy. But it is important to pick the minimum number of strategies as possible that will help one accomplish his or her mission. Not limiting ones strategies, will lead to complexity, which in some cases may turn out to be hard to achieve ones goals.

Secondly, reduce the number of tools you use. The greater the number of tools you use, may it be in your business or your workplace, the more complex your work will be. So it is better to try and combine some of the tools you use and try not to have the same information in different tools so as your work may be simple.

Thirdly, be determined to seek simplicity. For you to have an active to make things simpler, you must be determined and motivated. Accepting simplicity just because it is there is not just enough. You must move an extra mile. The drive and motivation to simplify things must come from your inner attitude. Devoting time, thinking energy, scheming effort and money in trying to make things simpler is very essential.

Fourth, you need to be prepared to start over and over again. Sometimes, trying to simplify some operational structures or modifying them becomes hard due to their complexity so you are forced to start from the beginning. Be clear on what you are doing and start it all over again ignoring the entire existing structure or system. Sometimes this is expensive and less likely to be accepted.

Fifth, you need to use concepts. The human mind simplifies things around by using concepts. The first stage of thinking in setting the general direction for purpose is provided by concepts.

Reward is a motivator that is given after a particular task is completed. After embracing simplicity you will actually enjoy benefits of simplicity. Some of the benefits of simplicity are;

- **Under-reacting**

When things get complicated or too busy, one tends to get lost in a reactionary lifestyle, give responses that one did not mean to and sometimes even blow up things totally out of control. When living a simple life, one is able to consider his/her response. Having time to reflect on what you are about to say helps you to reflect on it, appropriately from a thoughtful mindset.

- **Self-care**

Elimination of common stressors like hurtful relationships, debts and crappy jobs, reduction of commitments and obligations gives us an ample time to deal with our hearts and souls. It also gives space for meditation and gratitude practice.

- **Better Health**

Changing diets or doing exercise is not always a solution to living a healthy life. Sometimes simplicity is the solution. Simplicity can reduce the risk of diseases, stress and can even lower your blood pressure hence playing a major role in your health and fitness.

- **Massive freedom**

When we have better health, not engaged in dramas not feeling crappy or overreacting, we have massive freedom, which helps us to live the lives, we want and make the right decisions.

Lesson # 7: Control Your Living Expenses

Take a look at most of the successful people around you. Analyze the life of the CEO of your company, the top ten richest people in your state, and so on.

You will find out that they are living a life, which is in line with their levels of success and money supply.

Do not spend more than you earn! Such an act will only lead to more of lifestyle inflation. This type of lifestyle can also explain why most super-successful people like musicians and celebrities in the art industries end up in bankruptcy. Eventually, such people live in lower class houses while settling endless debts.

But Warren Buffett is different when it comes to checking his ego as far as lifestyle is concerned. Notably, one can conclude that the core values that he uses for his business and investments are the same that he applies when dealing with his personal finances.

He is well known for his simple tastes. During an interview with CNBC, he said, "Success is really doing what you love and doing it well. It's as simple as that. Really getting to do what you love to do every day - that's really the ultimate luxury…your standard of living is not equal to your cost of living."

Key Takeaway:

By checking on his lifestyle and living expenses, Buffett can survive during the instances of financial crisis. His **"CHECKED"** lifestyle ensures that he can avoid **"AVOIDABLE"** debts. Such debts are the main things that lead to most of the successful people's bankruptcy.

Warren Buffet does not spend money on relaxation, travelling and other ways that people use to forget the wretchedness of the day's job. He is contented in what he has in terms of standard living and he is not interested in new cars or bigger houses

Buffett lives a simple lifestyle that controls his spending. For example, he still lives in Omaha Nebraska in the same five-bedroom stucco house that he bought for $31,500 back in 1957. Certainly, the house is comfortable according to him, although not anywhere close to the "palaces" that many people who are as wealthy as Warren Buffett tend to stay.

<u>**Next Action Plan:**</u>

Buffett's lifestyle has got an adamant message. By regulating your expenses, you can go through tough economic times and have an unquestionable margin of safety. With an affordable rent, you will not need to change your flat when you lose your job or record a loss in your business.

Determine where you spend your money so that, in as little as one month, you can get a solid idea which will help you track on how you will be spending your money. As you continue, you will gradually come up with a strategy to develop and you will be able to address you living expenses amicably.

Remove unnecessary routine purchases. This may not be the largest saving area but it is essential and applicable. This may bring about some psychological strains but when you compute the money you had been using in unnecessary purchases, you will realize a very significant difference.

If you have made a big purchase, make sure for the next 24 hours or whichever amount of time you think is feasible and will make an impact, you are not going to spend. Therefore have a cooling off period after huge purchases.

Advantageously, budgeting your cash gives you control over your money. When you spend and save your money in an intentional manner, you are under a budget. With budgeting, one is able to know whether he or she is able to sacrifice his or her short-term frequent expense for a long-term benefit. Budgeting also saves one the stress of sudden adjustment due to lack of funds, since you had not initially planned on how to use them.

In addition, budgeting makes one aware of what is going on with his or her money. You are able to track your income, how and where it goes to with budgeting. It also makes you knowledgeable on what you can afford, then efficiently plan on how to lower debts and take advantages of buying and investing opportunities.

Budgeting enables you to organize your savings and spending. When you have divided your money into expenditure categories and savings, a budget can help you know exactly how much each category of expenditure is taking which helps in planning and controlling your living expenses.

Finally, budgeting provides you with an early warning of potential problems. When you have budgeted your money and developed a sequence on spending, you may be able to predict a future problem and you will be able to flexibly adjust, so as to evade the problem.

Lesson # 8: Learn the Art of Saying "No."

Sometimes in life it can be difficult to say "no", but you are to shield your own significances, it is a critical lesson to apply. It does not mean that you should discard the other party. It means that you are declining a specific request being made by a person, which will inconvenience you in one way or another.

In life, more so on your journey to success, you will meet diverse race of people. You will have to deal with people from different social classes and geographical locations. You will find yourself in a dilemma when someone asks you for something you have never done before, or something that you steer clear with but really might have interest with.

Although, successful people master the importance of saying "NO." Warren Buffett is no exemption on this. Don't cross your lines to make someone happy at your expense. This act will at the one-time cost you, your business, or capital.

"The difference between successful people and successful people is that successful people say no to almost everything." - Warren Buffett.

Key Takeaway:

Buffett has mastered the art of saying 'No' and this is the reason as to why he is successful. If he is not into something, the response is always a bold and confident "NO."

Many at times we overdo things in our daily lives. Overdoing things basically means that you are doing something to an undesirable extent. In a nutshell, this is mostly termed as overcommitting. Have you ever overcommitted? Do you over commit? Or rather have ones been a volunteer at some juncture? Sometimes we have a tendency of overcommitting. We sometimes have our priorities misplaced and misguided. As much as the human race is concerned, everybody has priorities during various stages in life. We should be able to first take care of the key areas of our lives. This means say no to those things that misplace or misguide your set priorities. Focus first on your priorities, be it God, your precious family, your job, your business and any other priority that you may have. When you are done with your priorities, you can choose whether to say no, to other miscellaneous activities that come in your way.

<u>Next Action Plan:</u>

Learn that 'Too Many Eggs in the Bag Will Burden Your Load." Know your limits and never go beyond them. If you don't like meetings like Buffett, there is no need to force yourself. This is an ultimate strategy for tremendous success in life and business.

It is important for one to be aware of the appropriate and inappropriate time and situations to say "no." some of the inappropriate time to say no are; when it is not the best move or when you are saying no for the sake that, is not a good idea to give a "yes." When you are in a new job, it is not good to jump in deductions and say "no", it is good first to wait and build up affiliations and learn the ropes before deciding to say no.

It is always good to value your time, know exactly how appreciated your time is, and know your obligations. This ensures when a person asks you to dedicate some of your time to new commitments, you will be able to decide whether or not to take the commitment. Even if you may be having some extra time, it is good to know your priorities. There are many ways you can say "no" in a gentle, respectful, and courteous manner. Remember that being respectful does not mean that you need to explain in detail why you are saying "no". Your "no" should be brief, polite and fairly works best. The way you may approach personal situations while saying "no" is different from the way you say "no" in a work situation.

Being unable to establish clear boundaries at work or at home since you were unable to say "no" can have some effects such as; being overburdened, fatigued, and feeling as though you are being taken advantage of. Saying no when it is a "no" directly reflects to value in your life in the following ways:

- **You will have more precious time for yourself**

Time flies like an arrow; fruit flies like a banana. — Anthony G. Oettinger

It is human nature that we tend to demand more time from other people's time. You must learn to say no since people will demand your time for you to be part of their business, leaving you wondering when you will have time for yours.

- **Authenticity.**

Authenticity is a collection of choices that we have to make every day. It's about the choice to show up and be real. The choice to be honest. The choice to let our true selves be seen. — Brené Brown

- **You will be more than twice as productive**

Being a victim of saying "yes" always than one should, suffers one productivity since most of your time is being dedicated to doing other people's obligations.

- **Making worthwhile decisions.**

In agreeing when you need to agree and disagreeing when you need to disagree, you give yourself a chance to rethink your decision, which turns out to be bold decisions.

Lesson # 9: Take Control of Your Time

Time is a resource. You can never recycle your time. It is a rather limited resource. Warren Buffett is a no time waster, just like the most super-successful people in the world. Time management is a key factor is their lifestyles. Warren Buffett to be specific, works within schedules and priorities. He has also mastered how to balance his time between his investments and family.

"Chains of habit are too light to be felt until they are too heavy to be broken." – Warren Buffett.

Key Takeaway:

Buffett has maintained his success in life by taking quality control between his business time and family time. To him both are important. Without his investments he can never provide for the family and similarly, without his family, nothing will motivate him to work extra hard.

Buffett strictly adheres to his schedules and does his duties in their designated time. He does not procrastinate hence the ability to make a successful man.

<u>Next Action Plan:</u>

Learn the importance of time management. You should also practice the art of good time management. You can make it a habit of working with priority lists. By so doing, you will be able to work on the things that count for you to succeed in life.

Time management sheds light on various points that should never be neglected in order to control your time effectively and efficiently;

- **Keeping away from multi-tasking**

Many people supposedly think that multi-tasking is a great way to get most of their work done faster and to make the best use of the limited time, but in real sense, multi-tasking makes your work last longer. It also makes the quality of work to come out shoddy, since one is not fully immersed in one task. This is where a to-do list is most important. Tackle each task at a time and give it sufficient time and concentration. Your quality of work will as a result be awesome, rather than trying to do over four tasks at once and you end up doing none perfectly.

- **Do not overcommit yourself.**

When you have committed yourself to way too many tasks, it comes out like you are struggling to gain control of your time. You should think about the things that you are doing for yourself, not the things that you are obliged to do. Basically, think about what really matters to you.

- **Get organized.**

One of the acts, which can really make you feel you are in control of how you spend your hours, is getting organized. Having things like; a planner, pens, a calendar and a clean notebook where you take down your to-do lists can help you feel less overwhelmed. Organizing yourself relives you the stress of looking for things without knowing exactly where they are. This saves you a lot of time and energy.

- **Avoid procrastinating.**

"Success is having the discipline to do what you are supposed to do even if you don't feel like doing it"- Todd Smith

Procrastination is the enemy for success. Procrastination can be avoided through; doing what you keep on procrastinating in the morning, if you keep on putting off a task, try doing it in the morning, make preparations i.e. by assembling the proper tools, commit yourself, doing first things first and reflecting on the great feeling you will get when you have finished.

- **Show up early.**

Rushing from one task to the next is one of the reasons that may make one feel as if they are not in control of their time and life. This usually makes one feel stressed and frazzled which in turn may create bad impressions to the people waiting for you. William Shakespeare once said that "Better three hours too soon than a minute too late" If you are always running late almost everywhere, try to space your commitments far enough.

- **Carve out alone time.**

Alone time helps you to get some meditation and gives you energy to take your next task obligation. So this time should be as important as the time you spend with your friends or relatives or other important people in your life. Make sure you have a date with yourself, do not allow anyone or anything hinder you from this time, since it is during this time that you should review yourself and check on your progress and make your next moves.

- **Get enough sleep.**

When we tend to get busy, we usually sacrifice sleep as the first option. Make sure you get enough sleep like 7 – 8 hours a night like the likes of Warren

Buffet and Bill Gates. You can never feel as if you are in control of your time if you do not get enough sleep. Make sure each day you sleep and wake almost at the same time for your body to get used to the sleeping pattern.

- **Eat healthy meals**

Eating should be a priority not an option. If you want to make the best of your day, make sure your breakfast robust, your lunch is invigorating and your dinner is nourishing.

- **Have time for exercise.**

Most of us when we are swamped up with loads of work we tend to sacrifice exercises. However, some exercises such as swimming gives us energy and strength to handle some complex tasks. Exercising relaxes both body and mind and reduces fatigue and stress hence keeping us in control of our time.

Lesson # 10: Take a Step at a Time

You cannot serve two-master at the same time. Even the simplest thing for example eating, requires patience. No matter how fast you eat; it has to be step by step. One bite after the other. This applies more in business. If you rush with business, you will easily get stuck. Managing one-step after the other is a must have principle for every businessman. If the likes of Buffett had not made a step at a time, seemingly you could not hear of the big titles such as most successful investor. It all took him time and resources to fill up all his gaps making him that rich. This phrase has also been sung in a song by Jordin Sparks. A step at a time will ensure that you don't "fall" on your way.

"I don't look to jump over 7-foot bars: I look around for 1-foot bars that I can step over." ~ Warren Buffett.

The journey to success is just like a ladder. Warren Buffett clearly understands this well; you climb a stair at a time. That explains why he ones used the above quote. He actually meant that he moves one step at a time in his operations or investments.

Key Takeaway:

Buffett has earned his life success by focusing on small wins. He takes a single venture at a time. Such investments end up piling up to create a super-successful stock investment portfolio. He also embraces this strategy in his family life.

<u>**Next Action Plan:**</u>

You can never have an overnight success. You will need **"BABY STEPS"** on your journey to success in life. Learn to venture in business and investments by taking small and manageable hops to your final goal. By so doing, you will avoid any adverse effects that would otherwise arise by venturing wholly in the business.

"Hurry Hurry has no blessing". Why would a person rush to make a lot of money in a quick way yet it only leads him into a hole? The money making process is procedural at any point. It does not matter which kind of wealth you possess. You have to move from one step to another.

The steps to be taken have to be essentially right and wise. You can opt to take one-step at a time, but all your doing is to take unwise steps that would not help you in the long run. As you choose your steps, you have to be well informed and knowledgeable of where they would land you. Success is a journey and a journey begins with a step.

Business Lessons

Lesson # 11: Have a Management that is Reputable

Generations of financial managers, analysts and investors have benefited from the world's most successful investor's brilliant style of management. Having portrayed some of the best and practically applicable management styles, he has indeed impacted a good number of managers globally. Warren Buffett vividly brings to your attention the real time investment and money management approach, which would definitely deliver handsome results to investors. He argues that, a continued preoccupation of short-term investment never works. When you take out all the variables of the investments such as taxes, and come to realize that a larger percentage of the funds are wasted in stock, it is no surprise that most financial managers turn out to have failed even in the average market returns.

Truly, who would share top-notch secrets on his strategies on how he achieves his impressive results? Some of Buffett's management methodologies are strongly guarded. In Buffett's popular letters, he protectively asserts that, "despite our candid policies we tend to discuss our actions in marketable securities only to an acceptable depth." He further continues to say that, "great investment ideas are seldom, top notch and subject to combative appropriation similarly to your valuables."

Buffett focuses more on the reputation and work of the management, unlike most of the investment analysts who concentrate on the company's specific assets, market position, numbers, and public sentiments.

"When a management with a reputation for brilliance tackles a business with a reputation for bad economics, it is the reputation of the business that remains intact." – Warren Buffett.

Buffett understands that the future of the company is in the management's hands. He understands that other metrics like specific assets and market position can change in the future.

Key takeaway:

As most people would base their arguments, quality is a must have in every kind of management from investments to productivity. Buffett is barely out of the fence in his management reputation. Interestingly, when Buffett buys a stock, he considers purchasing the company as a whole.

Buffett knows that with the right people at the management helm, the company will prosper and grow despite the challenges that it might be facing in implementing appropriate measures for a practical prosperity.

The success of any business would depend on how well the owner or manager ideally sheds light in equity and capital. Losing money every year for a company, is a clear show of a lack in returns on equity and returns in capital. Return on capital directly reflects on how well a company utilizes its available resources profitably. Yearly, Buffett in his report eagerly waits to know the business that earned good returns on equity without relying on debts.

<u>**Next Action Plan:**</u>

Have a management that is reputable, if you are an entrepreneur or businessperson. Focus on selecting the right people for the positions that are tasked to manage your company. This is a free ticket to successfully appreciate your company investments profitably.

Practically, having a full control of your equity and capital returns, is a sure way of ensuring a noticeable development in your investments. Achieving this without debts is a certain indication of how well you have managed to run your investment. One of the most reputable managers, Warren Buffett, argues the same way. He includes in his report that, for a manager to make a healthy profit on shares, he has to pick on companies that make a great return on equity and a huge return on capital.

If you are looking for a job opportunity, inquire much about the management of the company rather than the assets and salary. Knowing the tinniest detail of a company, places you in a better place of knowing the stability of the company now and in future. This trick should extend even to your investment decisions.

Lesson # 12: You Should Get Used To Risk

According to Buffett, risk is not volatile, but simply the chances of losing an initially made investment. If there is a high possibility of losing an initial investment then the risk is definitely inappropriate and you are highly not advised to pick or even consider it. "Risk comes from not knowing what you're doing." - Warren Buffett. He takes quite a number of risk for instance with his insurance companies. Risk in business entails the possibility of the business experiencing a loss, comparative to taking an anticipated profit. As far as business is concerned, we are in the business of taking risks as you can hardly predict the outcome of a business.

By conventional standards, Warren Buffett's way to wealth is perilous. Buffett does not invest his money heavily in safe assets like Treasury bills and bonds. He otherwise chooses to focus on investing in primary stocks. Although contrary to most of the people's opinions, main stocks are not as risky as many people think. Moreover, Buffett once clearly stated that as long as you are sure of what you are doing you will ultimately succeed in the venture and get paid appropriately. Before you make a decision to undertake a risk, you ought to clearly understand the risk. This is an obligation of every investor and financial institution at large.

Mostly, people tend to misjudge the future when taking risks in the company in which they invest. It happens to quite a number of managers. The big danger about investment is that you look at a company now and get surprised about what its future develops. Buffett in his speech justifies this, when he highlights about an investment he made on a shoe company and unfortunately fifteen years afterwards, produced nothing completely despite a very careful analysis.

Key Takeaway:

Risk is commonly weighed in terms of reward. Risks are quite pressurizing and stressful. The higher the perceived reward, the higher the risk. If you make one mistake in a huge risk, you immediately fall hence a possible collapse.

Warren Buffett gains the ability to reduce most of the risks that are associated with primary stocks by buying them cheaply. This act squeezes out the high prices and risk of failure out.

But takes position that will definitely yield, and that only a global financial crisis can make such stocks reduce in pricing. He buys when every other person has sold out. When the market is crashing, this is when Buffett buys his shares, giving him a high advantage in gaining from his incurred risks.

Next Action Plan:

You are a better manager for risk management for your firm and have a principle responsibility in the management. The Financial risks we often get ourselves into, are caused by various factors:

- Excessive debt.

A company would take risks as instruments to speed up time. It can be in need of owning particular assets instead of waiting for them later. For example a company wants to change its products, it would go ahead to take up a debt and speed up time instead of waiting for a particular period of time to change the products.

- Overpaying for an investment

Prices which you pay is the value of what you get. Assuming a prospective buyer gains a strong interest over a particular car costing two million dollars. He offers to buy it at a hundred thousand dollars more than its actual price. After some time the buyer wants to sell the car, and these car cannot be sold at its buying price as much as it is still in a good condition. The poor investment was based on quality and not the initial price paid. The buyer overpaid for the car not taking into consideration the value.

- Not knowing what you are doing.

Buffet insists on knowing the kind of risk you get involved in anytime you take a risk. Take actions that you understand the kind of risk involved in an investment.

Risk can never be entirely eliminated as long as you want to succeed in life and business. It can otherwise be reduced by calculating the chances with the lowest risk possible. If you are an employee, focus on companies and positions with the lowest risks possible regarding job security.

In any case, as an entrepreneur, learn to calculate risks, understand the kind of risk you are getting into and take into account the value of the risk. Do not venture into a perilous business like gambling, if you are not fully prepared to take the associated risk in case "the coin tosses unfavorably.

Lesson # 13: Losing Positions Are Best Sold In Strong Market

Buffett likes using examples in getting his points home. Categorically, he uses sporting examples most of the time. Once, he used the famous Ted Williams, a professional baseball player that, if he carved the strike zone into seventy seven cells, swinging at the balls in his best cells, he would bat four hundred, whereas aiming at balls in his worst spot, on a different side of the strike zone, he would reductively bat two hundred and thirty balls. Hence waiting for the best time to sell your stocks in a strong market would be making a million dollar move. In practice, make use of your losing positions by selling the in strong markets, where you are pretty sure of a handsome return. Buffett has correctly learned the art of selling the 'losing positions' in strong markets. He minimizes losses by waiting until the stock market is adamant so that he can sell the seemingly losing positions. At such a time, he even recoups some profit.

<u>Key Takeaway:</u>

Buffett focuses on making a profit even during tough financial times for the particular business. It is a concept that most investors find difficult in mastering. They actually hold the stock, while it starts rising in value with the notion that it will continue growing. Although, as far as Buffett is concerned a losing position can never change despite the current price.

For high maximization of profits, sell your products when the market is strongly in need of the product, and not when everybody is trying to sell his or her product. Selling your products at this time would actually mean you should sell your products competitively to appropriately fit potentialities in the market.

<u>Next Action Plan:</u>

Having in mind Buffett's point of selling your loosing positions in strong markets, you should make use of three useful steps. Firstly, get to know your home-run stock. The kind of stock whose price rises dramatically over a short period of time. Having noted this at the back of your mind helps you to know what type of stock to invest in. Secondly, you should have the knowledge of when the home run stock is good for exit. When all the criteria of making a great business avails itself, why not make the mega move? This is your time to act. Invest in a large amount of stock. Finally, you require confidence and most importantly knowledge. The power of knowledge becomes vital in this final step. Have real time knowledge on the behavior of home run stocks, thereby knowing when they are available. Confidence is a basic factor in this step, as it strengthens a person throughout the waiting time and during the huge investment. Every upright investor has an obligation of mastering the three useful steps of maximizing profits from buying stocks. Initially, finding out the home run stocks by ensuring they meet the criteria to be referred to as home run stocks. Next step being putting down the criteria for analyzing and understanding to avoid risks. Lastly is about knowledge and confidence for making wise actions. To sum up, you should not hold on a losing position. If you are in a startup where the market trend has changed (moving away from your business ideas) learn how to sell it, when you know some customers are not competitive.

Lesson # 14: Buy When Others Want To Sell

Buffett's strategies obediently follow the demand and supply patterns in the market. Selling when the demand is high and buying when the supply is high too. Quoting from the New York Times back in October 2008, Buffet's words were clearly focused to business lesson 14. "A simple rule dictates my buying: Be fearful when others are greedy, and be greedy when others are fearful. And most certainly, fear is now widespread, gripping even seasoned investors. To be sure, investors are right to be wary of highly leveraged entities or businesses in weak competitive positions. But fears regarding the long-term prosperity of the nation's many sound companies make no sense. These businesses will indeed suffer earnings hiccups, as they always have. But most major companies will be setting new profit records 5, 10 and 20 years from now."

Warren Buffett never runs with the herd. It is actually the trick to his success though the hardest thing to master. His philosophy in investment is, sell when all the other people are buying (be fearful), and buy when other people are selling (be greedy).

As per the Wall Street, this is the trick that the few successful stock investors follow. Actually, the rest of the crowd is commonly wrong.

Key Takeaway:

Buffett understands that when everyone want to sell, the cost of stock will go down. On the other side, when everyone want to buy, the price of the stock will go high even on some losing positions. He has also perfected the art of selecting the best stocks.

In my perspective, you would highly maximize profits if you make a point of selling when the demand is favorably high. This is Buffett's analogy on fear and greed. It is practically applicable in nearly all kinds of business that you might undertake, being conscious that you are looking to get a worthwhile value on payment of a price. The value gained from selling a product, is directly proportional to the revenue that the product will appreciatively give back.

Consequently, you should be able to predict the behavior of a market and a product in order to effectively and efficiently utilize Warren Buffett's analogy. You should have a business-oriented mind set in this. Become opportunistic and indeed you would appreciate good fruits of becoming greedy when others are fearful.

Most people tend to wonder when to sell stocks. This one of the things that Buffet really knows well. His intent is never to buy and sell stocks when it is high. Instead he buys stocks, to sell after a long period of time. It is under two major circumstances that you would find Buffet selling his shares irregularly. Firstly is when there is an expected return that is higher compared to another asset basing that the asset is being traded. Secondly, is in case the hosting company alters its fundaments. A company may also change its way of operation.

Next Action Plan:

Diversify your investment to the extreme. These would place you on a sure end, knowing that you a have your risks spread across various classes of assets. Diversification is a protection against ignorance. By buying when others are selling, you will have the ability to strike positions in strong businesses for fewer costs compared to what you would have paid when everyone is buying, and the market is running strong. Learn how to embrace this trick in business and investment and you will ultimately succeed in the same.

From Buffett's way of investing, every investor should take in his trick of buying and selling stocks. Aimless buying and selling leaves you in the same position you were at. For a successful investment, you should settle at long-term investments and sell when you need to sell and not when the prices go high, because that is definitely moving with the herd, which is very dangerous. Choosing a long-term investment will not give you pressure.

Lesson # 15: Always Avoid Fads

Just as discussed earlier, Buffet never flows with what everybody is doing. He strictly minds his own goals in business. It is an essential quality and lesson at the same time. Moving with what people do clearly shows a lack of focused objectives. Rarely would you find multi billionaires move with a herd simply because of the kind of drive that they proudly possess. The fact that Buffet does not move with the herd, or any trendy move that most investors undertake due to a particular handsome investment, fundamentally means that he will seldom go for stocks aimlessly, because investors are fashionably investing in a particular company.

Warren Buffett never invests in what all the other people are investing in. He never rushes for the **"HOT STOCK"** nor the best investments of the year. As mentioned above, Buffett will sell when the rest of the people are rushing to buy. He loyally sticks to his word that you get fearful when other people become greedy and vice versa.

For instance, Warren Buffett publicly acknowledged that he circumvents purchasing stock in the new social media companies like Google and Facebook. He has for numerous times cited that it will always be difficult for him to determine the value of such stock and 'rate' how they will cost in the future.

Key Takeaway:

One thing that we can learn from Buffett is that he is consistent with his investments. Whereas at times investing in fads might get him value and quality, he chooses to go with what he is used to. For a successful business operation, discipline in your investment pattern is very important. Generally, in most successful endeavors, one the root secrets is discipline. If you have established an investment pattern, stick to it. Do not move with the herd as most people blindly do. Buffet is well planned and discipline to his radius of competence in the investment styles that he puts into action.

Arguably, investment is not the amount of information that you boast yourself, on the contrary it is how pragmatically you utilize what you have no idea about. Buffett views this detailed understanding of the business operation to be an overview of a possible prediction of a future performance of the business. You have to deeply understand a business in order to be able to predict its future performance. This way you can be sure of maintaining a strong focus on your investment patterns.

Next Action Plan:

You should learn to focus on what you understand. If you are good in forex trading, then go with it. In any case, if you are good in business then go with entrepreneurship rather than investments. It becomes so disappointing; when you follow a particular decision made by people, when all you have is a glimpse of the idea that you have hurriedly invested into. And the worst happens when you end up in the losing end because of poorly and ignorantly following people's decisions. As a writer, in my perception, it is very much essential to have an established and well-organized investment plan to enhance organization and highly ensure a sure option in your investment decisions similarly to the most successful investor in the world, Warren Buffett. Steer clear with copying what the masses are doing. Learn to make your personal decisions and choices despite how opposing they are to the crowd's point of view, basing your argument on having a firm and arguable investment position.

Nevertheless, as mentioned earlier Buffett becomes so strict when it comes to financial measures. He sticks to returns on equity comparative to earnings per share. A very professional investment stand.

Lesson # 16: Work With Something Valuable

One of key Buffett's **"NEVER LOSE MONEY"** strategy is buying quality. He goes for value, as he understands this will determine how he will sell. Warren Buffett will never pay a full price for any investment; this includes the investments that have populated his portfolios. He has mostly picked on value at the expense of mere cash. Buffett spend his money philanthropically, in a well-calculated and selective manner. He bases his argument on value. I suppose, that Buffett would rarely make an investment in a mediocre organization. In his many featured investment decisions made, he has ventured in worthwhile kinds of investments.

Warren Buffett advocates for long-term investment. It is not because of any other reason, but actually the kind of value that is present in long-term investment. Besides, he prefers becoming greedy when people are fearful. Again I would with no doubts, direct this to value. Otherwise, he could be investing any time he feels like he should invest. That is not the case though. His investment patterns are rooted to the kind of value that is present in the venture he undertakes. Taking from lesson by lesson, a majority of lessons to be learnt are pointed toward value in the long run.

One of the ways he evades paying a full price is buying from the businesses and companies that sell at a discount. It is commonly known as value investing. Value investing entails the art of purchasing primary stocks in businesses that are undervalued in comparison to other companies in their industry.

Key Takeaway:

Buffett looks at the fundaments of business or company. He looks at its management, price-earnings ratio, revenue, earnings, dividend yield, return on equity, and such other metrics. He compares this to other metrics in similar companies and businesses. This justifies Buffet's option for valuable things. A company's value is criticized from the above-mentioned metrics. He carefully analyses the position of a company in terms of management, capital and equity returns amongst other mentioned variables. If the variables are favorable, he hugely invests in the particular company, which after a long term appreciates generously.

Buffett's value formula involves considering the most value for the least price. Value is basically the sum net earnings and the dividend. The net earning being the money that the company retain at the end of a financial year, used to grow the company. Informatively, the dividends are used to build an investor's portfolio.

Business or companies that are successful in management, capital and equity returns, revenue and price-earnings ratio, are somewhat strong in comparison to the competitors, but when it comes to their stocks they are way below them, such businesses become one of his investment candidates.

<u>Next Action Plan:</u>

Always focus on getting value. Value might be quite costly and difficult to get, but in the long run you would appreciate everything that comes with value itself. Remember that, when selling, the value will determine the sales compared to the other metrics. If you are an investor, look into the metrics of the company's balance sheet and income statements. Find out if they are faring well in business, but with underpriced stocks or bonds.

On a similar note, if you are in the entrepreneurship industry, learn the art of coming up with valuable products compared to your competitors. Worth is very essential in matters of price. An example, stocks have their varying prices at various financial times, the price of a stock ought to be as per the value created by the stock. Pick on your best stock option, then ensure that you determine the price of the second stock. Convince yourself that you need one stock more than the other, then calculate the best price.

Lesson # 17: Invest in Quality

Investing in quality means having a planned style of investment where you use a well-established criteria that aims at taking into account the clear company characteristics that make it sound like a quality company.

Buffett is a renowned top-notch investor with a brilliant reputation. Investing in quality is one of his pillars. It is not an easy task. It actually calls for extreme patience, a quality that most people tend to shy away from. Patience always includes perseverance in the long run. Investing in quality eminently means buying against the crowd or herd. You actually swim against the stream in order to catch quality stocks to invest in. Most retail investors opt to invest in short term investments. The short-term investments tentatively are not quality investments. This is because the amount of profit you get from short-term investment is a hand full. Short-term investments turn out to be so tricky in the long run. Most retail investors opt to invest in short term investments. A mistake that unfortunately, even professional investors find themselves making.

Investing in quality is among the Warren Buffett's Trademark investment strategies. Investing in quality implies that Buffett invests in companies with well-regarded products, companies that are well-known, and in companies with products that add value to the economy and consumer.

In most cases, Buffett invests his money in companies that have got household names. He understands that such companies have got strong base, brand recognition and market penetration.

Key Takeaway:

Unlike some of the less successful investors who are drawn to industries and companies they know nothing or little about, Buffett selects the companies that he fully understands and which have quality products and reputation. With quality, he is assured of a long-term inning investment and some earnings out of the deal. That is the precise meaning of quality investment.

Buffett deliberately goes for high-end investments. That is the reason for the title "best investor" worldwide. His sure techniques for investment make him better placed in terms of his worth. He has a huge cash possession that allows him to comfortably invest in large companies, and as a matter of fact, invest generously.

Next Action Plan:

You should never assume that the less you know about a venture, the more it will end up being a success. Learn the art of investing your money and venturing in quality companies and industries. You should work with an organization that sells well-valued products. In a glance, some of the vital factors that would guide you in making a big time investment decision entail:

- Focusing on quality companies

  Quality companies are the companies that from a detailed look, give a clear indication that they will last in the market for a reasonable period of time. Investing in such a company, gives an investor a peace of mind that his valuables are safely placed, and would benefit him in future.

- Making a long term investment

  While, short-term investments make money more quickly than long-term investments, they might be significantly posing the investor in higher risks. Besides, the short-term investments are differently taxed comparing with long-term investments. Another discouraging drawback about opting for short-term investment, is the high brokerage commission charged, which is an added expense hence disqualifying the investment. Moreover, most retail investors and some professional investors find themselves enclosed in this mistake, with barely a reversal way out. Picking on a long-term investment saves you a great deal from expenses to profits. That explains why top investors like Warren Buffett, prefer to take a long-term investment to a short-term investment.

- Going against the herd

  It is a hard but worthwhile decision altogether. I earlier stated that Buffet will never go with the herd. To handsomely enjoy investments, try out buying when other investors are selling, and selling when they are buying. Countable investors follow this principle. Buffett is very adopted to this principle.

- Picking on companies that have good management

With good management in a company, an investor is much convinced, that the particular company is going a long way. As a result, many investors rush for the well-managed companies due to the clear management gesture shown from the manner in which it is managed.

Lesson # 18: Your Success or Failure Is Your Responsibility

Who does not want success? Success is everybody's desire. From the smallest thing that we engage ourselves in our day-to-day activities, success is a key factor. Even that little kid out there goes to play and at the back of his mind, success blinks. Many at times you encounter uncertainties and a lot of sleepless nights. All in the name of the popular animal, success. It is always upon you. You as an individual have all the power to determine your success or failure. Success has various dimensions.

At the age of 25 years, Warren Buffett had already attained his childhood goal of financial freedom. He was $2 million rich. Today Warren boasts the most prestigious titles in the world. The world's greatest investor amongst other titles. Warren defines success as an inner provocation to proudly appreciate your efforts and continue developing your business. He justifies this lesson in his statement that, success is all about acquiring what you want, whereas happiness entails receiving what you require. One of the greatest statements by Buffett on success that makes my day, is not to critic yourself and your performance basing on what other people assume or think. This statement tentatively summarizes every detail about success.

There is a difference between understanding financial markets and being in the financial markets. Warren Buffett is in the commercial market because he understands them. He is aware of how stocks work. How stocks end up losing positions or gaining.

On the contrary, many less successful investors are in the financial markets, but they do not know how such markets work. It is the reason why most of them end up failing and losing their capital. It is all in their power to determine their failure or success!

Key Takeaway:

In his speech Buffett clearly stated, "As you move along in your career, you always want to consider your inner scorecard that is how you feel about your own performance and success. You should worry more about how well you perform rather than how well the rest of the world perceives your performance." This kind drive is just enough to keep you from a major success obstacle.

Buffett understands that whether he succeeds or fails in stock investment is his responsibility. Although, since he has chosen to succeed, he goes for the stocks that he fully understands. He opts to invest in the financial markets that he can analyze well and infer on whether they are candidates for his money or not. Warren Buffett advocates for the policy of learning everything about a given investment and then focusing on whether it is sound to invest on it or not. It is how a newbie investor will become an expert.

Next Action Plan:

If you are looking forward to succeeding in financial markets, then you should start by learning how such markets work. Learn about stocks, bonds, government securities, and so on. Learn about when they lose positions and when they gain. Find out how profits and losses of companies affect their stocks. It is in this way that you will be able to venture in a sound investment strategy. Summarily, success depends on the steps that you undertake.

A very essential success action plan that has placed Buffett on a prestigious ground entail:

Locating your heroes as they will never let you down. They will always have a very enormous impact on you. Your heroes will keep you motivated and focused in your success journey. Most vitally, have the right heroes. Those that have a behavior that inspires you in your success journey.

Secondly, your reputation is more important than money. We can afford to lose money but on the contrary we cannot afford to lose reputation. Reputation is a constant originating partly from your actions as an individual. You cannot judge your reputation yourself. It highly depends on the verdict of other people. It means that people might look at you and get a relative reputation to the behavior that you portray to them in your actions.

Other plans involve, hiring people of integrity and intelligence. This is an assurance that your job and tasks are in great hands and that you will barely find your work messed up. It is a success-boosting plan with no regrets. In addition, love your work. Passion is a very essential. Loving your job gives you a quality assurance all together in the whole working process. It is a great pillar in keeping you moving. Again, mistakes do occur. The biggest mistakes are those, which we do not see. Keep moving. People lose money here and there. Ones Buffett's manager reported a loss of $360 million but surprisingly; he gave a statement that no manager expects from his seniors. "We make mistakes". Tomorrow is another day. Be competitive. Make significant changes within yourself as you catch up with your progress on your road map to success. Keep reading too. Knowledge is power. Buffett reads 5-6 hours a day. Reading keeps you updated and knowledgeable.

Lesson # 19: Learn to Be In the Game for Long-Term

Giving up should never be a chapter in your mind. That moment you are about to give up is your ultimate moment of change. Everybody has ever experienced his share of temptation, either in his private life or in the company. Despite hardships, you should remain focused and motivated to new possibilities. Staying in the game for a long time never lets you down.

It is no doubt that Warren Buffett has been investing the financial market for a very long time. This long-term investment is a major contributor to his success and perfection as far as primary stock investment is concerned. Most of his investments are long term. At 10 years the great man had already placed a primary goal of financial independence. Interestingly, it has never changed. Buffett possesses companies that have for a very long time stay been in business. This includes both individually and via Berkshire Hathaway. Being up in the game for a long term does not do anything other than appreciating continuously.

When you have a look at the companies that are owned by Buffett including Berkshire Hathaway, they are all long-haul investments. Warren Buffett purchases stock and holds onto them for decades.

<u>**Key Takeaway:**</u>

Warren Buffett understands that as long as the business is unyielding, the venture will ultimately pay-off. He has mastered the art of tracking record, and sizes of his stock portfolios. These are some of the testaments for his success in stock investments. As I stated earlier, short term investments have quite a number of drawback, that If I were to invest today, I would definitely rush for a long-term investment. In a long-term investment, you have very little to worry about.

Warren considered things that happen weekly or monthly. He always kept it simple. At 11 years he bought his first stock at Apple Company in 1942. In his speech in an interview, he explains that, things are not rushing anywhere; not the country as well as the people. They will all grow in value over time. Do not believe the doomsayers. Stay focused in the game like Warren with the very long made investment. He looks for business investments, and looks at them in 10-15 years to come. He likes to be able to look at a company's history; earnings, consistency and can therefore correctly predict the company's future.

"Someone is sitting in the shade today because someone planted a tree a long time ago." - Warren Buffett.

<u>**Next Action Plan:**</u>

Think long and hard before you make an investment. Buffet considers very key factors before he takes a step of investing in a company. Some of the criteria that he employs, is looking at the company's earnings, history, and consistency amongst other factors. A company that has a solid history with a good track record, shows that it has been experiencing an upward growth over time, as a result a possible further growth in its future making it viable for investment. The financial performance is also vital. Stability in managing finance in a company is a good indication that the company will withstand its ground despite changes in the stock market. Consider whether the business has been up or down in the past recent financial years, its future investment plans and backup plans in catastrophic times amongst others.

Learn the art of investing in long-term using an established criteria. You should not focus only on changes in stock prices. If you can spend your money in a good company for long-term, you will definitely earn dividends annually.

Informatively, when starting a business venture, focus on companies that can assure you a long-term business. They include household products and such like. People will always need household stuff as long as humanity is in existence tentatively for eternity. A good example is the Coca-Cola Company.

Lesson # 20: Never Lose Money

It is a mindset that every businessman or investor ought to have. A large percentage of the world of investment is based on money making. It is a statement that many people would wish to say in their own context, "Making money is exciting". In deed it is exciting and nobody ever wants to lose money in any way! Warren speaks of it. He has made it look like it is one of the most important pillars of investment. His "rule number 1". Surely, never should you ever lose money, because you have all the power not to lose it. Every human was given a beautiful brain and energy to deliver stunning results.

I understand that "Never Lose Money" sounds rather awkward. Although, to make it simple for you, always take calculated risks. Warren Buffett, due to his success, can be termed as a 'PRO' in the field of taking calculated risks. He thoroughly assesses his money-making ways before making another step to invest.

"Rule No. 1: Never lose money. Rule No. 2: Never forget rule No. 1." – Warren Buffett.

Never venture into any business without understanding it correctly. As mentioned above, Warren Buffett always analyzes the company or industry and also benchmarks it against its competitors before considering investing on the same. Applying this analogy leaves you with a positive mind that you will not lose money and money will not lose you too!

Key Takeaway:

There is no way we can all never lose money as speculators but basically, we can do all we can never to lose money. When you lose money in an investment or a trade, you need to work out your ways to place you back on track. Be careful on your opportunity costs, in order to rarely lose money meaninglessly. Do your best not to lose money. Losing money costs you capital, time and effort that could be spent waiting for other high probability set ups and exits as Buffett states.

Buffett has never taken wild chances at any particular time. When it comes to his businesses, he has a specific criterion for investment. It is this strategy, which keeps him from entering in blind speculations.

Next Action Plan:

Losing money has never been my wish or your wish or even any other investing party's. In order not to lose money, consider confirming the claims in an investment. Taking for instance if something is guaranteed, you should make a point of knowing if it is guaranteed and know exactly what is guaranteed because it might unfortunately be unavailable and this would lead to a loss of money. As you take up the investment remember the first Buffett "rule" of never lose money. Being you have known the guaranties, may be if it were guarantee for money, you can get a direct access to go where the money comes from. A major step in acquiring certainty of your guarantees. Remember discipline, the key to most successful achievements. You should adhere to your principles and goals loyally. If you lose money, you do not only lose money but also time and even resources that will take you quite some time to recover from the loss of money.

By using the never lose money strategy as your baseline plan, it will have a very positive effect on everything that you venture in. Despite whether you are into investment or entrepreneurship, you will always earn something out of the venture. Most of the lessons above have outlined how Warren Buffett avoids losing money, from investing in quality to checking the reputation of the management.